THIS CALENDAR BELONGS TO:

_____

BeeU PUBLISHING

©2021 BeeU PUBLISHING. All rights reserved.
Contact: beeupublishing@gmail.com
If you liked this product, feel free to leave a review on purchasing site.

2022

Why Should you put your new calendar in the freezer?

To start off the new year in a cool way!

YEAR AT A GLANCE

JANUARY 2022

S	M	T	W	T	F	S
26	27	28	29	30	31	1
2	3	4	5	6	7	8
9	10	11	12	13	14	15
16	17	18	19	20	21	22
23/30	24/31	25	26	27	28	29

FEBRUARY 2022

S	M	T	W	T	F	S
30	31	1	2	3	4	5
6	7	8	9	10	11	12
13	14	15	16	17	18	19
20	21	22	23	24	25	26
27	28	1	2	3	4	5

MARCH 2022

S	M	T	W	T	F	S
27	28	1	2	3	4	5
6	7	8	9	10	11	12
13	14	15	16	17	18	19
20	21	22	23	24	25	26
27	28	29	30	31	1	2

APRIL 2022

S	M	T	W	T	F	S
27	28	29	30	31	1	2
3	4	5	6	7	8	9
10	11	12	13	14	15	16
17	18	19	20	21	22	23
24	25	26	27	28	29	30

MAY 2022

S	M	T	W	T	F	S
1	2	3	4	5	6	7
8	9	10	11	12	13	14
15	16	17	18	19	20	21
22	23	24	25	26	27	28
29	30	31	1	2	3	4

JUNE 2022

S	M	T	W	T	F	S
29	30	31	1	2	3	4
5	6	7	8	9	10	11
12	13	14	15	16	17	18
19	20	21	22	23	24	25
26	27	28	29	30	1	2

notes

JULY 2022

S	M	T	W	T	F	S
26	27	28	29	30	1	2
3	4	5	6	7	8	9
10	11	12	13	14	15	16
17	18	19	20	21	22	23
24/31	25	26	27	28	29	30

AUGUST 2022

S	M	T	W	T	F	S
31	1	2	3	4	5	6
7	8	9	10	11	12	13
14	15	16	17	18	19	20
21	22	23	24	25	26	27
28	29	30	31	1	2	3

SEPTEMBER 2022

S	M	T	W	T	F	S
28	29	30	31	1	2	3
4	5	6	7	8	9	10
11	12	13	14	15	16	17
18	19	20	21	22	23	24
25	26	27	28	29	30	1

OCTOBER 2022

S	M	T	W	T	F	S
25	26	27	28	29	30	1
2	3	4	5	6	7	8
9	10	11	12	13	14	15
16	17	18	19	20	21	22
23/30	24/31	25	26	27	28	29

NOVEMBER 2022

S	M	T	W	T	F	S
30	31	1	2	3	4	5
6	7	8	9	10	11	12
13	14	15	16	17	18	19
20	21	22	23	24	25	26
27	28	29	30	1	2	3

DECEMBER 2022

S	M	T	W	T	F	S
27	28	29	30	1	2	3
4	5	6	7	8	9	10
11	12	13	14	15	16	17
18	19	20	21	22	23	24
25	26	27	28	29	30	31

notes

JANUARY 2022

sunday	monday	tuesday	wednesday
26	27	28	29
2	3	4	5
9	10	11	12
16	17 Martin Luther King Day	18	19
23	24	25	26
30	31		

thursday	friday	saturday	notes
30	31 New Year's Eve	Jan 1 New Year's Day	
6	7	8	
13	14	15	
20	21	22	
27	28	29	

JANUARY 2022

27 monday

> I would lose weight for my New Year's resolution...but I hate losing.

28 tuesday

> An iPhone and a firework were arrested on New Year's Eve. One was charged and the other was let off.

29 wednesday

> Unfortunately I have two left feet, making it impossible for me to start the new year on the right foot.

30 thursday

> Did you hear about the guy who started fixing breakfast at midnight on December 31? He wanted to make a New Years's toast!

31 friday

> My New Years Resolution: 2560 X 1440p

New Year's Eve

1 saturday

New Year's Day

2 sunday

JANUARY 2022

3 monday

> What happened to the man who shoplifted a calendar on New Year's Eve? He got 12 months!

4 tuesday

> I had a crazy dream last night! I was swimming in an ocean of orange soda. Turns out it was just a Fanta sea.

5 wednesday

> A crazy wife says to her husband that moose are falling from the sky. The husband says, it's reindeer.

6 *thursday*

> Did you hear about the restaurant on the moon? I heard the food was good but it had no atmosphere.

7 *friday*

> I don't trust stairs because they're always up to something.

8 *saturday*

9 *sunday*

JANUARY 2022

10 *monday*

> A man sued an airline company after it lost his luggage. Sadly, he lost his case.

11 *tuesday*

> Never discuss infinity with a mathematician, they can go on about it forever.

12 *wednesday*

> My friend drove his expensive car into a tree and found out how his Mercedes bends.

13 *thursday*

> Yesterday, I accidentally swallowed some food coloring. The doctor says I'm okay, but I feel like I've dyed a little inside.

14 *friday*

> So what if I don't know what apocalypse means? It's not the end of the world!

15 *saturday*

16 *sunday*

JANUARY 2022

17 *monday*

> Some aquatic mammals at the zoo escaped. It was otter chaos!

Martin Luther King Day

18 *tuesday*

> The Middle Ages were called the Dark Ages because there were too many knights.

19 *wednesday*

> What do you use to cut a Roman Emperor's hair? Ceasers.

20 thursday

> My sister bet that I couldn't build a car out of spaghetti. You should've seen her face when I drove pasta.

21 friday

> I lost my mood ring and I don't know how to feel about it!

22 saturday

23 sunday

JANUARY 2022

> To the guy who invented zero, thanks for nothing.

24 monday

25 tuesday

> My friend's bakery burned down last night. Now his business is toast.

26 wednesday

> It's hard to explain puns to kleptomaniacs because they always take things literally.

27 thursday

> Two windmills are standing in a wind farm. One asks, "What's your favorite kind of music?" The other says, "I'm a big metal fan."

28 friday

> I can't believe I got fired from the calendar factory. All I did was take a day off!

29 saturday

30 sunday

JANUARY 2022

Why couldn't the bicycle stand up by itself? It was two-tired.

31 *monday*

1 *tuesday*

2 *wednesday*

I´ve been bored recently,
so I decided
to take up fencing.

The neighbors
keep demanding
that I put it back.

FEBRUARY 2022

sunday	monday	tuesday	wednesday
30	31	Feb 1	2
6	7	8	9
13	14 Valentine's Day	15	16
20	21 President's Day	22	23
27	28	Mar 1	2

thursday	friday	saturday	notes
3	4	5	
10	11	12	
17	18	19	
24	25	26	
3	4	5	

FEBRUARY 2022

31 monday

1 *tuesday*

> There was a kidnapping at school yesterday. Don't worry, though – he woke up!

2 *wednesday*

> I hate how funerals are always at 9 a.m. I'm not really a mourning person.

3 *thursday*

> I wasn't originally going to get a brain transplant, but then I changed my mind.

4 *friday*

> The guy who invented the door knocker got a no-bell prize.

5 *saturday*

6 *sunday*

FEBRUARY 2022

> What do you call an alligator in a vest? An investigator.

7 monday

8 tuesday

> Somebody stole all my lamps. I couldn't be more de-lighted!

9 wednesday

> I'm reading a book about anti-gravity. It's impossible to put down!

10 *thursday*

> What do you call a man with no arms and no legs stuffed in your mailbox? Bill.

11 *friday*

> Coffee has a rough time in our house. It gets mugged every single morning!

12 *saturday*

13 *sunday*

FEBRUARY 2022

> Why was the baby ant confused? Because all his uncles were ants!

14 *monday*

Valentine's Day

> I just found out that I'm color blind. The news came completely out of the green!

15 *tuesday*

> What should a lawyer always wear to a court? A good lawsuit!

16 *wednesday*

17 *thursday*

> Apple is designing a new automatic car. But they're having trouble installing Windows!

18 *friday*

> How do you make a good egg-roll? You push it down a hill!

19 *saturday*

20 *sunday*

FEBRUARY 2022

21 monday

President's Day

> The past, the present, and the future walk into a bar. It was tense!

22 tuesday

> What did the duck say when she purchased new lipstick? Put it on my bill!

23 wednesday

> Did you hear about that cheese factory that exploded in France? There was nothing left but de Brie!

24 *thursday*

> Did you hear about the guy who got hit in the head with a can of soda? He was lucky it was a soft drink!

25 *friday*

> What did the ranch say when somebody opened the refrigerator? "Hey, close the door! I'm dressing!"

26 *saturday*

27 *sunday*

FEBRUARY 2022

> England doesn't have a kidney bank, but it does have a Liverpool.

28 monday

1 tuesday

2 wednesday

Spring
is the perfect time
to turn over a new leaf.

MARCH 2022

sunday	monday	tuesday	wednesday
27	28	Mar 1	2
6	7	8	9
13	14	15	16
20	21	22	23
27	28	29	30

thursday	friday	saturday	notes
3	4	5	
10	11	12	
17 St. Patrick's Day	18	19	
24	25	26	
31	Apr 1	2	

MARCH 2022

28 monday

1 *tuesday*

> Why should you never trust a train? They have loco motives.

2 *wednesday*

> Towels can't tell jokes. They have a dry sense of humor.

3 *thursday*

> I wanted to take pictures of the fog this morning but I mist my chance. I guess I could dew it tomorrow!

4 *friday*

> Can February March? No, but April May.

5 *saturday*

6 *sunday*

MARCH 2022

7 monday

> What did the police officer say to his belly-button? You're under a vest.

8 tuesday

> What do you call it when a group of apes starts a company? Monkey business.

9 wednesday

> Why do bees have sticky hair? Because they use a honeycomb.

10 thursday

> A cabbage and celery walk into a bar and the cabbage gets served first because he was a head.

11 friday

> Want to know why nurses like red crayons? Sometimes they have to draw blood.

12 saturday

13 sunday

MARCH 2022

14 monday

> My boss told me to have a good day, so I went home.

15 tuesday

> Why do some couples go to the gym? Because they want their relationship to work out.

16 wednesday

> Why is Peter Pan always flying? Because he Neverlands.

17 *thursday*

> My wife asked me to go get 6 cans of Sprite from the grocery store. I realized when I got home that I had picked 7 up.

St. Patrick's Day

18 *friday*

> Why did the man fall down the well? Because he couldn't see that well.

19 *saturday*

20 *sunday*

MARCH 2022

21 *monday*

> How do celebrities stay cool? They have many fans.

22 *tuesday*

> Singing in the shower is fun until you get soap in your mouth. Then it becomes a soap opera.

23 *wednesday*

> Why are spiders so smart? They can find everything on the web.

24 thursday

> Why are frogs so happy?
> They eat whatever bugs them.

25 friday

> What did the flowers do when the bride walked down the aisle? They rose.

26 saturday

27 sunday

MARCH 2022

28 monday

> Stop looking for the perfect match...use a lighter.

29 tuesday

> What's red and smells like blue paint? Red paint.

30 wednesday

> My son asked me to put his shoes on, but I don't think they'll fit me.

31 thursday

> What does a clock do when it's hungry?
> It goes back for seconds.

1 friday

2 saturday

3 sunday

APRIL 2022

sunday	monday	tuesday	wednesday
27	28	29	30
3	4	5	6
10	11	12	13
17 Easter	18	19	20
24	25	26	27

thursday	friday	saturday	notes
31	Apr 1	2	
7	8	9	
14	15	16	
21	22	23	
28	29	30	

I lost my job at the bank on my first day.

A woman asked me to check her balance, so I pushed her over.

APRIL 2022

31 thursday

1 *friday*

> Why are so many people tired on April 1st? They just finished a 31 day March.

2 *saturday*

3 *sunday*

APRIL 2022

4 monday

> How do you weigh a millennial? In Instagrams.

5 tuesday

> I'm so good at sleeping, I can do it with my eyes closed.

6 wednesday

> What happens when you witness a ship wreck? You let it sink in.

7 *thursday*

> Why shouldn't you write with a broken pencil? Because it's pointless.

8 *friday*

> Why don't oysters donate to charity? Because they're shellfish.

9 *saturday*

10 *sunday*

APRIL 2022

11 monday

> Why was 6 afraid of 7? Because 7 ate 9.

12 tuesday

> What do you call a belt made of watches? A waist of time!

13 wednesday

> I want a job cleaning mirrors. It's something I can really see myself doing.

14 thursday

> What do you call a factory that sells generally decent goods? A satisfactory.

15 friday

> What do you call a pony with a sore throat? A little hoarse.

16 saturday

17 sunday

Easter

APRIL 2022

18 monday

> What do you do when you see a spaceman? Park in it, man.

19 tuesday

> What do you call a person with a briefcase in a tree? A branch manager.

20 wednesday

> I'm only familiar with 25 letters of the alphabet. I don't know why.

21 thursday

> Did you hear about the claustrophobic astronaut? Poor guy really needed some space.

22 friday

> Why did Cyclops close his school? He only had one pupil.

23 saturday

24 sunday

APRIL 2022

25 monday

> What did one wall say to the other? "Meet me at the corner!"

26 tuesday

> Did you hear about the beautiful wedding? Even the cake was in tiers.

27 wednesday

> What do clouds wear under their shorts? Thunderpants.

28 *thursday*

> Why did Mozart hate chickens? Because when he asked them for their favorite composer, they said, "Bach! Bach! Bach!"

29 *friday*

> Why did the snowman pick through a bag of carrots? Because he was picking his nose.

30 *saturday*

1 sunday

MAY 2022

sunday	monday	tuesday	wednesday
May 1	2	3	4
8 Mother's Day	9	10	11
15	16	17	18
22	23	24	25
29	30 Memorial Day	31	Jun 1

thursday	friday	saturday	notes
5	6	7	
12	13	14	
19	20	21	
26	27	28	
2	3	4	

My dad unfortunately passed away when we couldn't remember his blood type.

His last words to us were: ´´Be positive!´´

MAY 2022

28 thursday

29 friday

> April May get here sooner than you think.

30 saturday

1 *sunday*

MAY 2022

2 *monday*

> How much does the heaviest skeleton weigh? A skeleton.

3 *tuesday*

> How many ears do space aliens have? Three: The left ear, right ear and the final front ear.

4 *wednesday*

> Why did the invisible man turn down a job offer? He couldn't see himself doing it.

5 *thursday*

> Why did Cinderella get kicked off of the soccer team? Because she kept running from the ball!

6 *friday*

> What shivers at the bottom of the ocean? A nervous wreck.

7 *saturday*

8 *sunday*

Mother's Day

MAY 2022

9 *monday*

> The rotation of the earth really makes my day.

10 *tuesday*

> What do you call a person with no body and no nose? Nobody knows.

11 *wednesday*

> Why do ghosts love elevators? Because they lift their spirits.

12 thursday

> I sold my vacuum yesterday. It was just collecting dust.

13 friday

> Cosmetic surgery used to be taboo, but now when you talk about Botox no one raises an eyebrow.

14 saturday

15 sunday

MAY 2022

> Which school supply is king? The ruler.

16 monday

17 tuesday

> What can you do if you're scared of elevators? Take steps to avoid them.

18 wednesday

> How many bugs do you need to rent out an apartment? Tenants.

19 thursday

> Parallel lines have so much in common. It's a shame they'll never meet.

20 friday

> How do prisoners communicate with one another? Cell phones.

21 saturday

22 sunday

MAY 2022

23 monday

> What's the best part about Switzerland? The flag is a big plus.

24 tuesday

> What did one elevator say to the other? "I think I'm coming down with something."

25 wednesday

> You know what seems odd to me? Numbers that can't be divided by two.

26 thursday

> Why was the fraction worried about marrying the decimal? Because he would have to convert.

27 friday

> Two cannibals are eating a clown. One asks the other, "Does this taste funny to you?"

28 saturday

29 sunday

MAY 2022

30 monday

> What did the zero say to the eight? Nice belt!

Memorial Day

31 tuesday

> Evergreens might not mind winter, but for all the other trees, spring is a great re-leaf.

1 wednesday

A police officer just knocked on my door and told me my dogs are chasing people on bikes.

That´s ridiculous.
My dogs don´t even own bikes.

JUNE 2022

sunday	monday	tuesday	wednesday
29	30	31	Jun 1
5	6	7	8
12	13	14	15
19 Father's Day	20	21	22
26	27	28	29

thursday	friday	saturday	notes
2	3	4	
9	10	11	
16	17	18	
23	24	25	
30	Jul 1	2	

JUNE 2022

30 monday

31 tuesday

1 *wednesday*

> How do you make holy water?
> You boil the hell out of it.

2 *thursday*

Why do teenagers travel in groups of threes and fives? Because they can't even.

3 *friday*

I was wondering why the ball was getting bigger. Then it hit me.

4 *saturday*

5 *sunday*

JUNE 2022

6 monday

> "I have a split personality," said Tom, being frank.

7 tuesday

> I renamed my iPod The Titanic, so when I plug it in, it says "The Titanic is syncing."

8 wednesday

> Did you hear about the guy whose whole left side was cut off? He's all right now.

9 *thursday*

> Light travels faster than sound. That's why some people appear bright until you hear them speak.

10 *friday*

> Will glass coffins be a success? Remains to be seen.

11 *saturday*

12 *sunday*

JUNE 2022

13 monday

> When life gives you melons, you're dyslexic.

14 tuesday

> Heard about the new restaurant called Karma? There's no menu - you get what you deserve.

15 wednesday

> The man who survived pepper spray and mustard gas is now a seasoned veteran.

16 thursday

> My dad farted in an elevator, it was wrong on so many levels.

17 friday

> What's the difference between a hippo and a zippo? One is really heavy and the other is a little lighter.

18 saturday

19 sunday

Father's Day

JUNE 2022

20 monday

> What do you call a bee that can't make up its mind? A maybe.

21 tuesday

> I went to buy some camouflage trousers yesterday but couldn't find any.

22 wednesday

> When everything is coming your way, you're in the wrong lane.

23 thursday

> I told my husband yesterday that I hate June Bugs. He told me not to worry because they'll all disappear in July.

24 friday

> Jill broke her finger today, but on the other hand she was completely fine.

25 saturday

26 sunday

JUNE 2022

27 monday

> All chemists know that alcohol is always a solution.

28 tuesday

> When the past, present, and future go camping they always argue. It's intense tense in tents.

29 wednesday

> What did the janitor say when he jumped out of the closet? SUPPLIES!

JUNE 2022

I have a few jokes about unemployed people, but none of them work.

30 *thursday*

1 friday

2 saturday

3 sunday

JULY 2022

sunday	monday	tuesday	wednesday
26	27	28	29
3	4 Independence Day	5	6
10	11	12	13
17	18	19	20
24	25	26	27
31			

thursday	friday	saturday	notes
30	Jul 1	2	
7	8	9	
14	15	16	
21	22	23	
28	29	30	

A man walks into a bar
with a slab of asphalt
under his arm
and says:

*"A beer please,
and one for the road."*

JULY 2022

30 thursday

1 *friday*

> Is it ignorance or apathy that's destroying the world today? I don't know and don't really care.

2 *saturday*

3 *sunday*

JULY 2022

4 monday

What do you call the wife of a hippie? A Mississippi.

Independence Day

5 tuesday

What do you get when you mix alcohol and literature? Tequila mockingbird.

6 wednesday

How does an attorney sleep? First he lies on one side, then he lies on the other.

7 *thursday*

> Which country's capital has the fastest-growing population? Ireland. Every day it's Dublin.

8 *friday*

> A mean crook going down stairs = A condescending con, descending

9 *saturday*

10 *sunday*

JULY 2022

11 *monday*

> How do you throw a space party? You planet.

12 *tuesday*

> What are the strongest days of the week? Saturday and Sunday, the rest are weekdays.

13 *wednesday*

> The other day I tried to make a chemistry joke, but got no reaction.

14 *thursday*

> What's the difference between a poorly dressed man on a bicycle and a nicely dressed man on a tricycle? A tire.

15 *friday*

> Two fish are in a tank, one says to the other "how do you drive this thing?"

16 *saturday*

17 *sunday*

JULY 2022

18 monday

> How does Moses make coffee?
> Hebrews it.

19 tuesday

> I saw an ad for burial plots, and I thought: "That's the last thing I need!"

20 wednesday

> I used to be indecisive; now I'm not so sure.

21 *thursday*

> I was going to make a chemistry joke, but since I'm kinda late to the thread, the good ones argon.

22 *friday*

> What do you call the ghost of a chicken? A poultry-geist.

23 *saturday*

24 *sunday*

JULY 2022

25 monday

He who laughs last thinks slowest.

26 tuesday

Hal: How did you get hit on the head with a book? Sal: I only have my shelf to blame.

27 wednesday

I stayed up all night to see where the sun went. Then it dawned on me.

28 thursday

> C, E-flat, and G walk into a bar. The bartender shows them the door and says, "Sorry, we don't serve minors."

29 friday

> I'm on a seafood diet. Every time I see food, I eat it.

30 saturday

31 sunday

AUGUST 2022

sunday	monday	tuesday	wednesday
31	Aug 1	2	3
7	8	9	10
14	15	16	17
21	22	23	24
28	29	30	31

thursday	friday	saturday	notes
4	5	6	
11	12	13	
18	19	20	
25	26	27	
Sep 1	2	3	

AUGUST 2022

1 monday

> I'm not a doctor but I'm losing my patience.

2 tuesday

> I'm a big fan of whiteboards. I find them quite re-markable.

3 wednesday

> Be kind to dentists. They have fillings too, you know.

4 *thursday*

> A photon checks into a hotel. The front desk asks if it has any luggage. It replies "no, I'm traveling light".

5 *friday*

> I'm glad I know sign language, it's pretty handy.

6 *saturday*

7 *sunday*

AUGUST 2022

8 monday

> What do you call a dog on the beach in the summer? A hot dog!

9 tuesday

> Why aren't depressed people worried about flat tires? They're always carrying despair.

10 wednesday

> My friend David just had his ID stolen. We just call him Dav now.

11 *thursday*

> Why do Buddhist monks avoid sending word documents? They're supposed to avoid attachments.

12 *friday*

> Did you hear about the banker who left her job? She just lost interest.

13 *saturday*

14 *sunday*

AUGUST 2022

15 monday

> I refuse to work with compost, it's degrading.

16 tuesday

> What did the grape say when it got crushed? Nothing, it just let out a little wine.

17 wednesday

> I keep trying to start exercising, but it just isn't working out.

18 thursday

> How did the picture end up in jail? It was framed!

19 friday

> Did you hear that Magnesium formed an oxide layer? OMg!

20 saturday

21 sunday

AUGUST 2022

22 monday

> To be frank... I'd have to change my name.

23 tuesday

> I knew a guy who collected candy canes, they were all in mint condition.

24 wednesday

> Why are two helium isotopes so funny? HeHe!

25 *thursday*

> Did you hear about the man who called his doctor's office because he'd turned invisible? Sadly, nobody could see him for weeks.

26 *friday*

> Why did the ghost cross the road? To get to the Other Side.

27 *saturday*

28 *sunday*

AUGUST 2022

29 monday

> I bought a boat because it was for sail.

30 tuesday

> I nearly bought a clock today but it wasn't the right time.

31 wednesday

> Dyslexic prisoners are not helped by long sentences.

Did you hear about the
man who swallowed
six small plastic horses?

Doctors described
his condition as "Stable".

SEPTEMBER 2022

sunday	monday	tuesday	wednesday
28	29	30	31
4	5 Labor Day	6	7
11	12	13	14
18	19	20	21
25	26	27	28

thursday	friday	saturday	notes
Sep 1	2	3	
8	9	10	
15	16	17	
22	23	24	
29	30	Oct 1	

´´Doctor help!
I´m shrinking!´´

´´Take this
and you 'll be back
to normal in a few weeks.
Until then,
you 'll just have to be
a little patient.´´

SEPTEMBER 2022

A cross-eyed teacher couldn't control his pupils.

1 *thursday*

2 *friday*

Being in debt attracts a lot of interest from bankers.

3 *saturday*

4 *sunday*

SEPTEMBER 2022

> Religious lions get down on their knees to prey.

5 monday

Labor Day

> Double-glazing installation is easier to schedule with a big window.

6 tuesday

> Snowboarders who become dependent on drugs go downhill fast.

7 wednesday

8 *thursday*

> Successful corrective surgery on mermaids depends on the detailing.

9 *friday*

> For a furniture corporation to succeed it needs a good chairman.

10 *saturday*

11 *sunday*

SEPTEMBER 2022

Poorly run fishing companies have a net loss.

12 monday

13 tuesday

Airlines process missing luggage complaints on a case-by-case basis.

14 wednesday

Winemaking after a poor grape harvest can be fruitless.

15 thursday

> I'm on a c food diet; candy, cookies, and cake. My brother said carrots, cauliflower, and celery are c food too. I asked him who taught him to spell.

16 friday

> A big computerized dog needs a megabyte.

17 saturday

18 sunday

SEPTEMBER 2022

Old bikes should be retired.

19 *monday*

20 *tuesday*

There was a sign on the lawn at a drug re-hab center that said 'Keep off the Grass.'

21 *wednesday*

Napoleon may not have designed his coat, but he did have a hand in it.

22 thursday

> Did you hear about the Buddhist who refused Novocain during a root canal? His goal: transcend dental medication.

23 friday

> Iron man = Fe-male?

24 saturday

25 sunday

SEPTEMBER 2022

Clones are people two.

26 *monday*

27 *tuesday*

Thanks for explaining the word "many" to me. It means a lot.

28 *wednesday*

I once ate a watch. It was time consuming.

29 thursday

> Do you know that tadpoles are natural story tellers? It's just sad that when they get older, they lose their tales.

30 friday

> Two antennas got married. The ceremony wasn't much, but the reception was excellent.

1 saturday

2 sunday

OCTOBER 2022

sunday	monday	tuesday	wednesday
25	26	27	28
2	3	4	5
9	10 Columbus Day	11	12
16	17	18	19
23	24	25	26
30	Halloween 31		

thursday	friday	saturday	notes
29	30	Oct 1	
6	7	8	
13	14	15	
20	21	22	
27	28	29	

A neutron walks into a bar.
''I' d like a beer''
he says.

The bartender promptly serves up a beer.

''How much will that be?'' asks the neutron.

''For you?''
replies the bartender,
''no charge.''

OCTOBER 2022

29 thursday

30 friday

1 *saturday*

2 *sunday*

OCTOBER 2022

> I met my wife on a dating site. We just clicked.

3 monday

4 tuesday

> Knowing how to pick locks has opened a lot of doors for me.

5 wednesday

> I couldn't remember how to throw a boomerang. Eventually it came back to me.

6 *thursday*

> I quit my job at the donut factory.
> I was fed up with the hole business.

7 *friday*

> Architects are good at coming up with concrete plans.

8 *saturday*

9 *sunday*

OCTOBER 2022

10 monday

I tried to draw a circle, but it was pointless.

Columbus Day

11 tuesday

A friend said he didn't understand cloning. I told him that makes two of us.

12 wednesday

Getting paid to sleep would be my dream job.

13 thursday

> What happened when the semi-colon broke grammar laws? He was given two consecutive sentences.

14 friday

> I had a pun about amnesia, but I forget how it goes.

15 saturday

16 sunday

OCTOBER 2022

I gave away my dead batteries, no charge.

17 *monday*

18 *tuesday*

I'm designing a reversible jacket. I'm excited to see how it turns out.

19 *wednesday*

A cartoonist was found dead. Details are sketchy.

20 thursday

> My kid swallowed some coins, the doctor told me to just wait. No change yet.

21 friday

> After the birth of your child, your role in life will become apparent.

22 saturday

23 sunday

OCTOBER 2022

24 monday

> A backwards poet writes inverse.

25 tuesday

> Life as a professional yo-yoer has its ups and downs.

26 wednesday

> I used to hate facial hair, but it grew on me.

27 thursday

> Why was King Arthur's army too tired to fight? It had too many sleepless knights.

28 friday

> I failed my Braille class. It's a touchy subject.

29 saturday

30 sunday

OCTOBER 2022

> I decided to get rid of my spine. It was holding me back.

31 monday

Halloween

1 tuesday

2 wednesday

My wife refuses to go to a nude beach with me.

I think she's just being clothes-minded.

NOVEMBER 2022

sunday	monday	tuesday	wednesday
30	31	Nov 1	2
6	7	8	9
13	14	15	16
20	21	22	23
27	28	29	30

thursday	friday	saturday	notes
3	4	5	
10	11 Veterans Day	12	
17	18	19	
24 Thanksgiving	25	26	
Dec 1	2	3	

NOVEMBER 2022

31 monday

1 *tuesday*

> Accidentally buried someone alive. It was a grave mistake.

2 *wednesday*

> Why did the tomato blush? Because it saw the salad dressing.

3 *thursday*

> I got fired as train engineer. They tallied up all my accidents, it was so hard to keep track.

4 *friday*

> I used to be addicted to soap, but I'm clean now.

5 *saturday*

6 *sunday*

NOVEMBER 2022

7 monday

> Why couldn't the sesame seed leave the poker table? He was on a roll.

8 tuesday

> Did you hear the rumor about peanut butter? I'm not telling you. You might spread it.

9 wednesday

> Why are dogs bad storytellers? Because they only have one tale.

10 thursday

> What did the librarian say when the books were a mess? We ought to be ashamed of ourshelves.

11 friday

> The shovel was a ground-breaking invention.

Veterans Day

12 saturday

13 sunday

NOVEMBER 2022

A criminal's best asset is his lie ability.

14 monday

15 tuesday

I cut my finger shredding cheese, but I think I may have grater problems.

16 wednesday

I used to be a shoe salesman, until they gave me the boot.

17 *thursday*

> Why shouldn't you tell a secret on a farm? Because the potatoes have eyes and the corn has ears.

18 *friday*

> Which is faster, heat or cold? Heat, you can catch cold.

19 *saturday*

20 *sunday*

NOVEMBER 2022

21 monday

> Why couldn't the coffee go out? It was grounded.

22 tuesday

> No matter how hard you push the envelope, it will still be stationery.

23 wednesday

> I just heard they won't be making rulers any longer.

24 thursday

If you ever feel cold just stand in a corner. They're usually around 90 degrees.

Thanksgiving

25 friday

To solve claustrophobia you have to think outside the box.

26 saturday

27 sunday

NOVEMBER 2022

One lung said to another... we be-lung together!

28 monday

29 tuesday

Sure, I drink brake fluid. But I can stop anytime!

30 wednesday

My leaf blower doesn't work, it just sucks.

Two Eskimos sitting in
a kayak were chilly,
so they lit a fire
in the craft.

Unsurprisingly it sank,
proving once again that you
can't have your kayak and
heat it too.

DECEMBER 2022

sunday	monday	tuesday	wednesday
27	28	29	30
4	5	6	7
11	12	13	14
18	19	20	21
25 Christmas Day	26	27	28

thursday	friday	saturday	notes
Dec 1	2	3	
8	9	10	
15	16	17	
22	23	24	
29	30	31 New Year's Eve	

Every soccer player's favorite beverage?

Penal-tea!

DECEMBER 2022

> Two egotists started a fight. It was an I for an I!

1 *thursday*

> Who is the penguin's favorite aunt? Aunt-Arctica!

2 *friday*

3 *saturday*

4 *sunday*

DECEMBER 2022

5 monday

> Two peanuts walk into a bar, and one was a salted.

6 tuesday

> Two termites walk into a bar. One asks, "Is the bar tender here?"

7 wednesday

> An invisible man marries an invisible woman. The kids were nothing to look at either.

8 *thursday*

> Did you hear someone brought a sled to the downhill ski race? They let it slide!

9 *friday*

> Why do eggs hate jokes? The answer cracks them up!

10 *saturday*

11 *sunday*

DECEMBER 2022

12 monday

> I made a pun about the wind but it blows.

13 tuesday

> Waking up this morning was an eye-opening experience.

14 wednesday

> Never trust an atom, they make up everything!

15 *thursday*

> Two hydrogen atoms meet. One says "I've lost my electron," The other says, "Are you sure?" The first replies "Yes, I'm positive."

16 *friday*

> Getting the ability to fly would be so uplifting.

17 *saturday*

18 *sunday*

DECEMBER 2022

19 *monday*

> What washes up on tiny beaches? Microwaves.

20 *tuesday*

> Long fairy tales have a tendency to dragon.

21 *wednesday*

> How do you know that Santa is an expert at karate? He has a black belt.

22 *thursday*

> Asked my wife what she wanted for Christmas and she told me nothing would make her happier than a diamond necklace. So I gave her nothing.

23 *friday*

> I bought my son a refrigerator for Christmas - I can't wait to see his face light up when he opens it.

24 *saturday*

25 *sunday*

Christmas Day

DECEMBER 2022

26 *monday*

> What is it called when a snowman has a temper tantrum? A meltdown.

27 *tuesday*

> Did you hear the forecast for Christmas Eve? They're calling for rain, dear!

28 *wednesday*

> Carol called. She wants her off-key back.

29 *thursday*

> What happened to the man who shoplifted a calendar on New Year's Eve? He got 12 months!

30 *friday*

> Not to brag, but I already have a date for New Year's Eve. It's December 31st.

31 *saturday*

1 sunday

New Year's Eve

New Year's Day

JANUARY 2023

sunday	monday	tuesday	wednesday
Jan 1 New Year's Day	2	3	4
8	9	10	11
15	16 Martin Luther King Day	17	18
22	23	24	25
29	30	31	Feb 1

thursday	friday	saturday	notes
5	6	7	
12	13	14	
19	20	21	
26	27	28	
2	3	4	

NOTES

NOTES

NOTES

NOTES

NOTES

Printed in Great Britain
by Amazon